What's a PENGUIN D·O·I·N·G in a PLACE LIKE THIS?

Miriam Schlein

What's a PENGUIN DOING in a PLACE LIKE THIS?

The Millbrook Press   Brookfield, Connecticut

Cover photograph (front and back) courtesy of Animals Animals
© G. L. Kooyman

Photographs courtesy of Comstock, Inc.: pp. 2 (© 1994), 27 (© 1995), 29 (© 1992), 32 (© 1992); National Science Foundation, Office of Polar Programs: pp. 5 (Russ Kinne), 8 (Ann Hawthorne), 49 (Ann Hawthorne), 50 (Ann Hawthorne); Animals, Animals: pp. 6 (© Malcolm Coe), 9 (© G. L. Kooyman), 16 (© 1994 Maresa Pryor), 18 (© B. G. Murray, Jr.), 21 (© A. Bannister), 22 (© Zig Leszczynski), 35 (© Leonard Lee Rue III), 37 (© G. L. Kooyman), 43 (© G. L. Kooyman), 52 (© G. L. Kooyman); P. Dee Boersma, H. S. Center for Educational Resources, University of Washington: pp. 11, 12; Peter Arnold, Inc.: pp. 17 (© Jeffrey L. Rotman), 25 (© Bruno P. Zehnder), 62 (© Luiz C. Marigo); Frans Lanting-Minden Pictures: pp. 26, 30, 33, 53, 54; New Zealand Department of Conservaion: pp. 39 (R. Morris), 40 (R. Morris), 41 (R. Morris), 42; Australia Tourist Commision: p. 46.

Library of Congress Cataloging-in-Publication data
Schlein, Miriam
What's a penguin doing in a place like this? / Miriam Schlein.
p. cm.
Summary: Outlines the varied worldwide habitats, differences, and common traits of all kinds of penguins.
ISBN 0-7613-0003-1
1. Penguins—Juvenile literature. [1. Penguins.] I. Title.
QL696.S473S34 1997
598.4'41—dc20 96-28803 CIP AC

What kind of bird is a penguin?

It's a strange kind of bird.

Penguins don't fly—at least not through the air. But they're great swimmers and divers. Instead of wings, they have hard, flat flippers.

Like all birds, penguins have feathers. In fact, they have more feathers than any other kind of bird—up to 300 feathers per square inch! But their feathers don't look "feathery." They're so flat and smooth and dense, they look more like fur than feathers.

What Kind of BIRD is a PENGUIN?

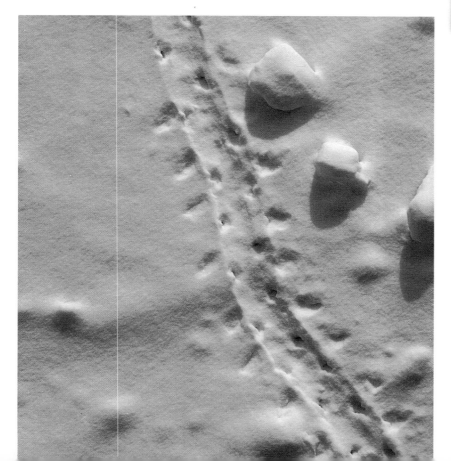

Can you believe a bird made these tracks? "Tobogganing" through the snow is one way that penguins get around.

Penguins don't fly through the air like most birds, but their sleek bodies and strong flippers make them excellent swimmers.

On land, penguins seem awkward. They waddle along, their barrel bellies supported on stubby legs. But once they hit the water, they're not awkward at all. Torpedo-shaped and sleek, they cut through the water. They speed along, propelled by their flippers, which they flap up and down in a flying motion. You could say penguins do "fly"—through the water.

To build up speed, they "porpoise." They break through the water's surface, are almost airborne for a moment while they take a fast breath, then plunge down again. In short spurts, they may reach a speed of 20 miles (32 kilometers) per hour. Their cruising speed is about 5 miles (8 kilometers) per hour.

The penguin's tail and stubby legs are used together as a rudder for steering. A penguin can change direction in an instant. By zigzagging back and forth it can escape a pursuing enemy—a leopard seal, an orca (killer whale), a shark, or an octopus.

Sometimes, people look at penguins and say, "Aren't they cute? They look like they're all dressed up in tuxedos!"

True, a penguin's black back and white front does look a bit like a tux. But this coloring is one more thing that helps to protect it. Seen from above, a penguin's dark back is less visible against the dark water below. From below, the white front makes it less visible against light from the sky.

A loud voice and flapping flippers bring attention, whether a penguin is looking for a mate or trying to find its group.

Most birds have light, hollow bones. This makes it easier for them to fly. Penguin bones are solid and heavy, which makes it easier for them to dive. Some penguins can dive to a depth of 1,000 feet (about 305 meters) and stay under water for about twenty minutes.

Penguins certainly don't "sing like a bird." They hiss and quack, they growl and trumpet. Some bark like a dog, or bray, "HEE HAW," like a donkey. A loud call helps a penguin at sea find its group again if it becomes separated. It also helps a penguin find its mate or chick in a crowded colony.

All the qualities that make penguins such unusual birds are the things that make them so well designed for their life in the sea.

Lots of people think all penguins live surrounded by ice and snow—that this is the "penguiny" way of life.

Is that true?

No.

There are 17 different kinds of penguins.

Not all of them live in ice and snow.

In fact, most of them don't.

Penguins are found in many different kinds of places—sometimes where you'd never expect to see them.

A FALSE IDEA *about* PENGUINS

Against a dramatic backdrop of snow and ice is where many people expect to find penguins, but most do not live in regions like this.

PENGUINS on the PRAIRIES

If you were standing at the water's edge at a certain time of year in a certain spot on the coast of Argentina, you would see a surprising sight: hundreds of little black-and-white heads bobbing through the water, heading toward the beach.

They're penguins. And they're traveling fast.

As they hit the beach, they may lie there for a bit, panting and resting. Then they get up and waddle off, heading for higher ground.

You're in Patagonia—on the prairie lands in southern Argentina. This spot, called Punta Tombo, is a spit of land that juts out into the ocean.

Two ostrich-like rheas run by. A llama-like guanaco is nibbling on a bush. Off in the distance, you might see some sheep.

What are penguins doing in a place like this?

It's their traditional nesting ground; the place they come back to every year to mate, lay their eggs, and bring up their chicks. Many have been swimming almost 2,000 miles (over 3,200 kilometers) to get here.

The penguins start to arrive in September. This is early spring in Argentina. They get to work right away. Most of them make nests underground in long burrows, which they dig out with their beaks and claws. They line the nest with twigs and feathers and bits of grass.

The mother penguin takes the first shift incubating the eggs (usually two), sitting over them to keep them

warm. Then the father takes his turn. After five or six weeks the chicks peck their way out. A chick has an egg tooth at the tip of its beak to help break the shell.

Now the mother and father penguin take turns, one guarding the chicks, the other going into the ocean to get food to feed them. They carry the food back in their

Penguins of Punta Tombo splash through the water toward shore to the nesting ground that they return to year after year.

Penguin parents take turns caring for their chicks—first sitting on the eggs, then going for food.

stomachs. Sometimes they are so overstuffed that they lose their balance and flop over as they waddle back.

The chick sticks its beak into the parent's mouth. The parent regurgitates, or spits up, bits of fish, and that's how the chick is fed.

Guanaco and sheep wander through the colony. They don't bother the penguins. But there are also dangerous predators hanging around—foxes, pampas cats, armadillos. Sometimes one will try to grab a chick. Most likely it will get slashed by a parent penguin's razor-sharp bill. But sometimes a prowling predator is able to grab an unlucky penguin chick.

By autumn the chicks are fledged. They've shed their fluffy baby coats, and have grown dense water-proof feathers. They're ready now to go into the sea and swim off with the others. The penguins spend months in the ocean, feeding and fattening up until it's time once again to head back to Punta Tombo.

Dee Boersma is a scientist who has been studying these penguins. By banding thousands of them (clipping on identification bands), she has learned that they swim up along the coast of Brazil, some traveling as far as the waters off Rio de Janeiro. That's a swim of about 1,800 miles (almost 2,900 kilometers). Their enemies at sea are orcas, sea lions, and seabirds called giant petrels.

The penguins of Punta Tombo are a species, or group, called MAGELLANIC PENGUINS, named after the explorer Ferdinand Magellan. About half a million nest in the Punta Tombo colony. The total Magellanic population is more than a million.

How to identify a Magellanic penguin
(*Spheniscus magellanicus*):

2 black stripes across chest.

Height: 20 inches
(51 centimeters)

Weight: 11 pounds
(about 5 kilograms)

WHERE PENGUINS *live*—AND *do not* LIVE

Look at this map. You will notice two things right away:

- Penguins are found only south of the equator. That's right—no penguins live at the North Pole.

- Also, many penguins nest on small islands. Why is that?

Penguins are safer on islands. Usually on islands there are few, if any, predators. This is why flightless birds—birds that can't escape an enemy by flying away, as other birds do—are almost always found on islands.

There are some exceptions: The ostrich of Africa, the emu in Australia, and the rhea of South America are nonflying birds that do not live on small islands. But they are fast runners, and have a different way to escape—by running away.

That's what makes Punta Tombo such an unusual nesting area. It's not a safe little island. It's part of the mainland, and various predators are there.

Why do the penguins nest there? No one is sure of the answer.

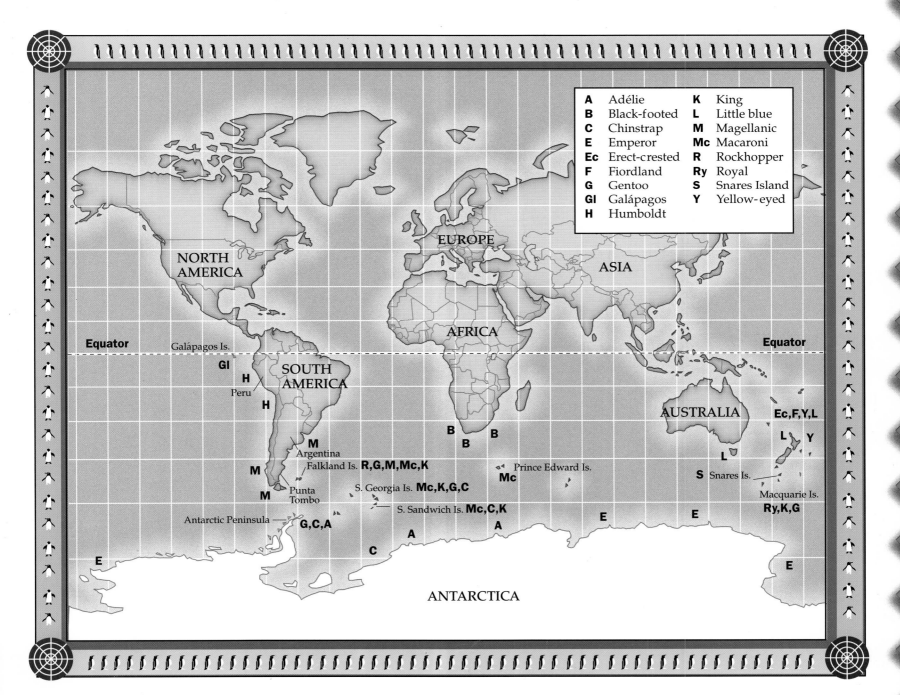

PENGUINS *on a* TROPICAL ISLAND

Did you know that there are penguins that live on a tropical island?

The Galápagos Islands, off the coast of Ecuador, are close to the equator. The temperature there is usually over 100°F (38°C). It's not the kind of place you would expect to find penguins. Yet there they are.

Like all penguins, GALÁPAGOS PENGUINS have dense, warm, waterproof feathers. How do they manage to stay cool in such a hot part of the world? One thing they do is spend the hot sunny days in the water, and come up on land at night, when it's cooler.

But there are times when penguins cannot go into the water: when they're incubating eggs, and also when they're molting. This is the time when their old, worn feathers fall out and they're waiting for new feathers to grow in. The penguins then take shelter in black lava rock caves by the sea.

There are other special things that penguins do to cool off. They raise their feather tips to let air come through. They pant like a dog, which gets rid of body heat. They also lie down and expose the soles of their feet to release body heat. The soles of its feet are one of the few areas where a penguin has no feathers.

Galápagos penguins do not gather in large colonies. Just two or three pairs may nest together in a cave.

A Galápagos penguin rests on a cool rock. Penguins often spend the hottest part of the day in the water.

Marine iguanas are one of the many species that share the Galápagos Islands with penguins. They may look scary but are no danger to the penguins.

How to identify a Galápagos penguin (*Spheniscus mendiculus*):

Black stripe across chest.

Height: about 15 inches (38 centimeters)

Weight: about 5 pounds (2.3 kilograms). It's one of the smallest penguins.

They have some unusual neighbors on the islands: marine iguanas 4 feet (1.2 meters) long, 500-pound (227-kilogram) land tortoises, and blue-footed boobies. Sometimes you will see a penguin perched on a rock close to a bunch of iguanas. They don't seem to bother one another.

Galápagos penguins do have enemies in the sea to watch out for, such as sharks, seals, and giant red crabs.

The total Galápagos penguin population is between 6,000 and 15,000.

PENGUINS *in* PERU

South of the Galápagos Islands are more small islands off the coast of Peru. These are the home of the HUMBOLDT PENGUINS.

These islands used to be covered with guano—droppings of pelicans and other seabirds. In some places the guano was 100 feet (30 meters) deep. The penguins dug burrows in the guano and nested there. It was a safe place. And there was another plus. The surrounding waters were swarming with anchovies, which made a good food supply for the penguins.

The islands that are home to the Humboldt penguins were once covered with the guano of seabirds, like those pictured with the penguins here.

Then catastrophe hit. In the 1800s, people discovered that guano was a terrific fertilizer. They began removing it by the boatload. Also, the waters around the islands were overfished. So the penguins lost two important things: their nesting area and much of their food supply. Many also drowned when they were accidentally trapped in fishing nets. Now there are fewer than 10,000 Humboldts left. They nest in rock caves by the sea.

Humboldt penguins are named after the Humboldt Current, which flows through these waters. They're also called Peruvian penguins.

How to identify a Humboldt penguin
(*Spheniscus humboldti*):

Black stripe across chest.

Height: 19 inches
(48 centimeters)

Weight: About 9 pounds
(4 kilograms)

PENGUINS of Southern AFRICA

"There are birds as big as ducks, but they cannot fly because they have no feathers on their wings. . . . These birds bray like asses. . . ."

In 1497 a sailor named Alvero Vello wrote those words in his diary. He was sailing around the southern tip of Africa with explorer Vasco da Gama.

The birds he saw were penguins. But how could he know that? At that time, no Europeans had ever seen such a bird.

He was wrong about their not having feathers, but Vello was right about one thing: These birds *did* bray like asses, or donkeys.

The birds he saw were BLACK-FOOTED PENGUINS. Their calls sound so much like a donkey braying that they are sometimes called "African jackass penguins." They live in the waters off the coast of southern Africa, where they dart about eating squid and small fish. They seldom swim more than 5 or 6 miles (8 to 10 kilometers) from shore.

Black-footed penguins nest mostly on small offshore islands, though sometimes they're found on the mainland. Using their beaks and claws, they dig burrows in the sandy soil. There the mother penguin lays her pale-green eggs (usually two, but sometimes three or four).

Like some other species of penguins, black-footed penguins sometimes climb rocks to get to their nesting grounds on the mainland.

Black-footed penguins are found mainly on the islands off south-west Africa; about 20 inches (51 centimeters) tall, they are of average size for penguins.

Like all penguins, the mother and father share the job of protecting and feeding the chicks. On land, they have to guard against airborne predators such as gulls and ibises. Enemies in the sea are sharks and octopuses.

Black-footed penguins are unusual in that they raise two clutches, or families, every year. Most penguins breed only once a year.

Their population is between 120,000 and 150,000. All four of the species of "warm-weather penguins" (Galápagos, Humboldt, black-footed, and Magellanic) hee-haw like a donkey, or jackass. For this reason scientists have grouped them in a genus sometimes called JACKASS PENGUINS.

Warm-weather penguins almost always have bare, unfeathered areas on the face, which makes it easier for them to cool off. Their feathers are shorter and not as closely packed as those of other penguins.

How to identify a black-footed (African jackass) penguin
(*Spheniscus demersus*):

Wide black stripe across chest and down sides, pink mark above eyes.

Height: about 20 inches (51 centimeters)

Weight: about 6.5 pounds (3 kilograms)

A PENGUIN PARADISE

The Falklands are a clump of islands off the tip of South America. In Argentina they are called the Malvina Islands.

The islands are windy and bare. There are no trees, only low-growing diddledee bushes and tough tussock grass. Not many people live there. But lots of penguins do. Each species stakes out its own space.

The first penguins you might see are ROCKHOPPER PENGUINS. Rockhoppers are peppy little penguins. They pop up out of the sea, land on a rocky ledge, and shake themselves off. Then they get moving.

Holding their feet together, they hop upward from rock to rock. You can see how they got the name "rock-hoppers." One penguin follows the next, follow-the-leader-style. In particularly steep places, they grab onto the rock with their beaks and dig in with their claws.

They are heading up to the cliffs 600 feet (183 meters) above the sea. There they build nests of sticks and feathers and grass.

They lay two eggs. The second egg is bigger than the first. Often the parents are not able to provide enough food for two chicks. So only one—the chick from the larger egg—will survive. This is true of some other species as well.

The mother and father share the job of getting food for the chick, going back and forth, up and down the rocky trail.

In about three weeks the little brown chick leaves the nest and joins a crèche—a group of chicks tended

Rockhopper penguins are named for their amazing ability to scramble over rocky beaches and scale the cliffs that stand between them and their nesting grounds.

How to identify a rockhopper

(*Eudyptes chrysocome*):

A crest of bright-yellow head-feathers above the eyes sticks straight up when the bird is excited; red eyes, red beak, pinkish feet.

Height: 16 inches (41 centimeters)

Weight: 5 pounds (2.3 kilograms)

The rockhopper's bright-yellow crest identifies it as one of many species of crested penguins.

by a "baby-sitter." In nine or ten weeks the chicks are fledged and independent, able to enter the sea.

Rockhoppers gather in large colonies, sometimes more than a million together. The total rockhopper population, in the Falklands and in other areas, is between 3.5 and 4 million.

Some GENTOO PENGUINS also nest in the Falklands. They gather on grassy meadows where they make bowl-shaped nests out of twigs. Their colonies are small—no more than a few hundred pairs together.

The timid gentoo is unlike other penguins in that it does not return to the same nesting area year after year.

How to identify a gentoo penguin

(*Pygoscelis papua*):

White splotch over eyes, long feathery tail, red beak, pale-pink feet.

Height: 22 inches (56 centimeters)

Weight: about 13 pounds (6 kilograms)

Gentoos are timid. If a person comes close, a rock-hopper will strike out with its beak. But a gentoo will often retreat. Unlike most penguins, gentoos usually do not return every year to the same nesting area.

Some Magellanic penguins are also found in the Falklands. Unlike the Punta Tombo Magellanics, they gather here in small groups—maybe four or five pairs together. They choose an area with soft soil, where they can dig out nest holes.

Near the sea, small groups of king penguins gather. And up on the rocky slopes, there is still another species of penguin. There are only a few. They look a lot like rockhoppers, except they're bigger. But they have the same red eyes, pinkish feet, and bright, wavy head-feathers.

They are MACARONI PENGUINS.

Are these pasta-eating penguins?

How did they get that name?

In London in the 1700s, there was a group called the "Macaroni Club." It was a bunch of trendy young fops—fancy dressers who had elaborate hairstyles and wore hats with colorful, wavy plumes. When English sailors saw these penguins with bright head-feathers, they were reminded of those Macaroni characters back home. That's how these penguins got their name.

MILLIONS OF *Macaronis*

Macaroni penguins seem to live up to their name. Macaronis were a group of Englishmen in the 1700s who were flashy dressers.

How to identify a macaroni penguin

(*Eudyptes chrysolophus*):

Orange or yellow head-feathers,
red eyes, red beak.

Height: 20 inches
(51 centimeters)

Weight: about 9.5 pounds
(4.3 kilograms)

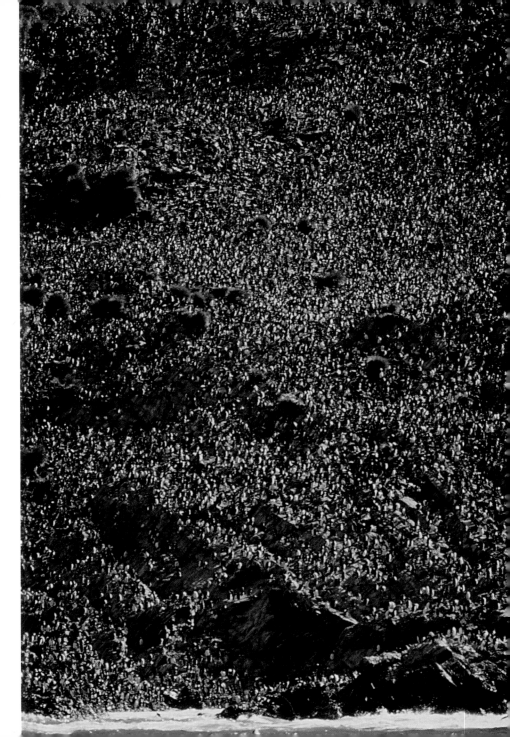

How many macaronis are on South Georgia Island? Maybe millions!

To see millions of macaronis, the place to go is South Georgia Island, about 800 miles (1,287 kilometers) from the Falklands. It's a cold, rocky, and bleak island. Its only occupants are penguins.

They arrive in early summer. Like rockhoppers, macaronis are skilled climbers. High on the rocky slopes, often 500 feet (152 meters) or more above sea level, macaronis by the millions make nests out of pebbles and rocks. There they lay their eggs and raise their chicks.

Why do they nest so high up? In low areas, close to sea level, the nest might be flooded. The eggs could be washed away, or the young chicks drowned.

By mid-summer, the macaroni chicks are fledged. They are only two months old. But they are already able to climb down, leap into the ocean, and fend for themselves.

The total macaroni population is about 25 million. They nest on many of the small islands that dot the southern oceans.

A MESSY, *Smelly* PLACE

South Georgia Island also has large colonies of KING PENGUINS. Kings are easy to identify because of their bright-orange "earmuffs."

King penguins stand straight and tall; they have a rather dignified posture. But their colony is anything but dignified. It is often located in mud, at the foot of a melting glacier. It is smelly, messy, muddy, and noisy.

King penguins, among the largest penguins, stand tall and seem like royalty.

King penguins do not build a nest. The mother lays a pale-green egg on her feet. The mother and father take turns incubating the egg, holding it under their warm belly feathers. Each time they pass the egg to one another, they make a ceremony of it. They wave their flippers, raise their heads, and give out trumpeting greetings.

It takes about eight weeks for the egg to hatch. At first the king chick is a naked, helpless little thing. But after about three weeks, it gets its fuzzy coat of brown down, and joins a crèche. It takes a much longer time

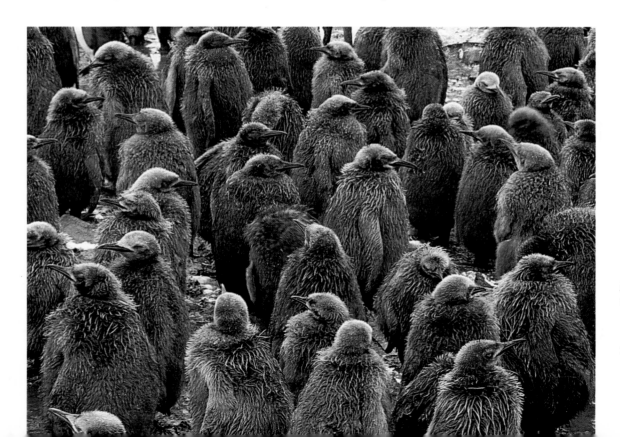

The fuzzy brown king penguin chicks in this crèche may look big enough to be on their own, but they take longer to fledge than most other penguin chicks.

How to identify a king penguin

(*Aptenodytes patagonicus*):

Bright orange ear patches, long pointy beak, bluish-gray back.

Height: 28 inches
(71 centimeters)

Weight: up to 40 pounds
(18 kilograms)

than most penguin chicks—about a year—before the king chick is fledged. Over the winter, there may not be enough food to feed the chick. Sometimes months go by without the chick being fed. If the chick doesn't have a good reserve of body fat, it may not survive.

King penguins breed only twice in three years, rather than every year, as most penguins do. The total king population is probably more than two million.

Some gentoo and chinstrap penguins also make South Georgia Island their home base. The gentoos make nests in the high tussock grass, using whatever building material they can find: feathers, seaweed, pebbles. The chinstraps nest in small groups, up on the rocky slopes.

There are many more CHINSTRAP PENGUINS—about two million of them—on the South Sandwich Islands, a group of small islands that lie farther below the South Georgia Islands. The mountains here are covered with glaciers. High on the icy slopes, the chinstraps make nests out of stones, bones, and feathers. Sometimes the nest wall is high enough to act as a windbreak. Chinstrap chicks don't gather in crèches.

THE *South Sandwich* ISLANDS

In its rocky nest high on a slope, a chinstrap penguin parent cares for its two chicks.

How to identify a chinstrap penguin

(Pygoscelis antarctica):

Thin black "strap" under chin, long feathery tail, black beak, pinkish feet.

Height: 20 inches
(51 centimeters)

Weight: about 10 pounds
(4.5 kilograms)

Most penguins remain in the nesting area as they molt, but chinstraps sometimes don't wait: They molt as they travel through the sea on drifting icebergs.

Chinstraps are aggressive: They hiss and stamp their feet and often charge if threatened. Their calls are so loud that these penguins are sometimes called "stone crackers."

Chinstraps also nest on other islands, and on the Antarctic Peninsula. Their total population is about 15 million.

In the melt and the mud at the foot of the South Sandwich glaciers there are also small colonies of king penguins.

There is only one place in the world where ROYAL PENGUINS nest. That is on Macquarie Island, a small island south of Australia.

CAN a *Macaroni* be **ROYAL**?

Royal penguins (sometimes called Macquarie Island macaronis) arrive once again to nest and raise their chicks, splashing as they go.

**How to identify
a royal penguin**
(*Eudyptes schlegeli*):

Orange or yellow crest,
top of head black,
face and neck white.

Height: 19 inches
(48 centimeters)

Weight: 9 pounds
(4 kilograms)

The climate is mild. The hills are covered with wild grass. Every summer all the royals in the world come from the sea to nest here.

Some stay close to the shore. Others go inland, following little streams, splashing along until they get to their traditional nesting area.

Royal penguins are closely related to macaronis. They are different in only one way: Macaronis have a black face and neck; royals have a white face and neck. Some scientists say that the royal should not even be considered a different species, but a subspecies, or variation, of the macaroni. They believe that, instead of "royal," this penguin should be called the "Macquarie Island macaroni."

Some kings and gentoos also nest on Macquarie Island. They stroll around on the black sand beaches, close to clumps of elephant seals.

New Zealand is an island-country southeast of Australia. The climate is mild. The coastline is broken by fiords—long inlets that cut into the shore. This is the home of more species of penguins.

FIORDLAND PENGUINS feed in the sea in the daytime, and come up on land at night. They nest in the rain forest, in caves, and under vines. They stay in small groups, or sometimes just one pair by itself.

PENGUINS *of* NEW ZEALAND

Peeking out of the nest it has built in a cave, a fiordland penguin protects its eggs.

How to identify a Fiordland penguin

(*Eudyptes pachyrhynchus*):

Yellow "eyebrows," thick, pale brownish-orange bill.

Height: 16 inches
(41 centimeters)

Weight: 6.5 pounds
(3 kilograms)

Hidden away in the forest are other flightless birds. One is the kiwi. Another is a parrot called the kakapo. One that penguins have to watch out for is the weka, which steals penguin eggs when it can.

Fiordland penguins also nest on small nearby islands. Their total population is between 10,000 and 20,000.

SNARES ISLAND PENGUINS nest on one small island south of New Zealand. They stay in the scrub, or brush, and in swampy areas, and build nests out of guano and grass. These penguins sometimes roost on low tree

Snares Island penguins usually nest in swampy, grassy areas. They are closely related to fiordland penguins.

This Snares Island penguin may be calling out to a mate, or it may be trying to frighten off a seabird that has its eye on one of the penguin's chicks.

How to identify a Snares Island penguin
(*Eudyptes robustus*):

Wispy crest, thick pale-orange beak with small featherless area at the base.

Height: 16 inches
(41 centimeters)

Weight: 6.5 pounds
(3 kilograms)

branches. The Snares Island penguin is similar to the fiordland penguin. Some scientists say it is not a separate species, but a subspecies of the fiordland penguin.

Their main enemies are sea lions, which gather on nearby beaches. Skuas will also try to snatch a penguin chick or an egg.

Their total population is about 66,000.

How to identify an erect-crested penguin

(*Eudyptes sclateri*):

Short stand-up crest, orange beak, pale-pink feet.

Height: 20 inches
(51 centimeters)

Weight: 8 pounds
(3.6 kilograms)

THE ERECT-CRESTED PENGUIN has a short bristly crest that sticks straight up like a brush. These penguins nest on islands off the New Zealand coast, where they gather in large colonies on beaches, on rock ledges, or in muddy areas. They often swim in groups of hundreds, and keep track of each other by barking. Their total population is about a half million.

The erect-crested chick in this picture has the familiar penguin coloring, but has not yet developed its yellow crest.

Erect-crested, Snares Island, fiordland, macaroni, royal, and rockhopper penguins are all in the genus of CRESTED PENGUINS.

Crested penguins have red eyes and yellowish plumes. Except for the fiordland penguin, they spend long, unbroken periods of time (up to five months) in the sea.

The YELLOW-EYED PENGUIN has—you guessed it—yellow eyes. It also has a band of yellow on its head.

The habitat of the yellow-eyed penguin has diminished, and so has its population. Only a few thousand are left in the world.

How to identify a yellow-eyed penguin

(*Megadyptes antipodes*):

Yellow eyes, yellow band over head, pinkish beak.

Height: 19 inches
(48 centimeters)

Weight: 11 pounds
(5 kilograms)

These penguins nest on islands south of New Zealand, and also on the mainland, sometimes not far from a city. If a dog or any other intruder comes sniffing around, the yellow-eyed penguin will send it off with a squawk and a smack of its flipper.

These penguins once nested in rain forests along the coast. But bit by bit much of their habitat has been cut down. Now they nest in small groups or isolated pairs, on hillsides and in gullies, sheltered from the sun by boulders and cliffs.

Yellow-eyed penguins do not spend long periods of time in the sea. They usually go into the water by day, and come back on land at night.

The sea lion is their main enemy in the water. Yellow-eyed penguins are also killed when they get entangled in large fishing nets. On land their enemies are cats, dogs, ferrets, and pigs.

Their total population is dangerously low, between 2,000 and 5,000.

Australia is the home of the smallest penguin of all. It's called the LITTLE BLUE PENGUIN.

In the daytime these mini-penguins dart about eating sprats and other small fish. Unlike most penguins, little blue penguins have more enemies on land than in the sea: rats and cats, lizards and snakes, as well as airborne predators like gulls, skuas, and eagles. The penguins come up on land at night, under cover of darkness. In the morning, before dawn, they head back into the sea.

Near the city of Melbourne, floodlights have been set up on a strip of land where the penguins come out of the sea. Crowds gather every evening to watch them come up and march single file to their nesting spots. The presence of people doesn't even seem to bother the penguins.

Some little blue penguins dig burrows 5 feet (1.5 meters) long to nest in. They line the nest with seaweed and grass. Others nest under bushes or in rock crevices. Sometimes they gather in colonies of a few thousand pairs. But often they nest just a few in one spot, or even in isolated pairs.

Mother and father share the job of incubating their two eggs. For three weeks after hatching, the chicks are guarded by one parent or the other. After that, the chicks are left alone in the nest. In eight weeks they have their waterproof feathers, and are ready to swim off on their own.

Parade of the LITTLE *blue* PENGUINS

Near Melbourne, Australia, a parade of little blue penguins is a major attraction. The penguins seem not to mind the spectators as they march to their nests.

Often, both chicks survive through the fledging period. This is unusual among penguins. Once in a while a pair of little blue penguins may even raise a second family in the same year. Like the yellow-eyed penguins, little blue penguins usually stay in the same waters all year round.

Mostly, they nest on offshore islands. But some nest on the mainland. This puts them in one kind of danger that most penguins do not face: being run over by a car or truck.

Sometimes a pair decide to nest under a house. It might seem like fun to have penguins under your house. But they can be pretty noisy. They growl and quack. They trumpet and hiss. They bleat like sheep. Not much fun when you're trying to sleep.

Little blue penguins are also found in New Zealand. The little blue penguin is sometimes called the fairy penguin, or dwarf penguin. Their total population is several hundred thousand.

How to identify a little blue penguin
(*Eudyptula minor*):

Gray-blue feathers, blue beak, white throat, pink feet.

Height: 11 inches
(28 centimeters)

Weight: 2.5 pounds
(a little over 1 kilogram)

Antarctica: a Most UNLIKELY NESTING PLACE

Antarctica is where we expect penguins to be. But if you think about it, it's really a most unlikely place.

It's the coldest place on Earth. It's covered with snow and ice. Nothing grows there. No trees. No grass. And except for tiny insects found under rocks, nothing can live there year round. Yet this is the place—the only place—where two species of penguins return every year and remain to breed and raise their chicks.

October is the beginning of spring in Antarctica. That's when the ADÉLIE PENGUINS start to arrive. The first few pop up out of the water. If there is a high ice ledge at the water's edge, they leap up, grab hold with their toenails, and pull themselves up. Soon there are millions of them, getting ready to nest.

Like other male penguins, the male Adélie does what is called display. He stands with his beak pointed upward. He waves his flippers slowly, and calls out "kronk, krooonk." Adélies often return to the same "neighborhood" of the same colony as the year before.

A female joins him. Most likely, it is his mate from the year before. Adélies usually seek out the same mate year after year. Facing one another, toe to toe, the two penguins sway their heads back and forth and wave their flippers. This is their courtship before mating.

They build a nest of little rocks. They carry these, one at a time, in their beaks. There's a lot of competition for rocks. The penguins fight over them. They bump each other. They whack each other with their flippers, and they bite.

This male Adélie penguin, hoping to attract a mate, puts on a showy display.

An Adélie parent sits on its rocky nest guarding the newly hatched chicks.

Finally, the nest gets made. It's not soft. But it does keep the eggs from rolling away. As with all penguins, the father and mother share the job of incubating the eggs, and feeding and guarding the chicks.

If there is a blizzard, the snow may get so deep that the penguins can end up in a snow hole 2 feet (0.6 meter) deep. But they don't desert the nest.

When a chick is about three weeks old, it joins other chicks in a crèche. Their "baby-sitter" must be watchful. A skua may swoop down and try to snatch a chick. Usually the skua is chased away by a peck from the sitter's sharp beak.

As a chick gets bigger, it needs more and more food. Sometimes a chick is still hungry, and the parent has no food left. The parent runs off, with the chick dashing after it. This is called a feeding chase. Penguin parents will feed only their own chicks. If both of a chick's parents are killed, no other penguin will feed it. It will die of starvation, or be eaten by a skua.

At eight weeks, the chicks lose their fluffy down. They gain their black and white waterproof feathers—and their independence. They walk to the water's edge and dive in. This is an important time. They practice swimming, diving, and getting their own food—mostly small, shrimplike krill.

It's also a dangerous time. A leopard seal, with its big mouth and sharp teeth, might be lying in wait. This is something that young penguins don't know. So for some, it's their first and last dive. More than half the chicks don't survive their first season.

Meanwhile, on shore, the adults are molting. By now, winter is approaching. It's time for the Adélies to go back to sea, where they stay for about five months, fattening up on fish and krill. Sometimes they hop up to ride on a drifting ice floe. This is a way to escape an orca or leopard seal. In the spring, the Adélies return once more to their nesting grounds to raise a new generation of chicks.

Adélie penguins were given their name by a French explorer, Admiral Jules Sebastian César Dumont D'Urville, who named them after his wife.

Adélies, chinstraps, and gentoos have long, feathery tails that trail behind them as they walk. They are in the genus called LONG-TAILED PENGUINS.

How to identify an Adélie penguin
(*Pygoscelis adelie*):

Solid black head, long tail, thin white line around eyes.

Height: 20 inches
(51 centimeters)

Weight: 9 pounds
(4 kilograms)

ROUTINE
of the
EMPEROR PENGUINS

The EMPEROR PENGUIN—the biggest penguin—also breeds only in Antarctica. In fact, most emperor penguins never set foot on the land itself. On the sea ice—10 to 15 feet (3 to 4.5 meters) thick—that forms on the ocean around the shore, the emperors gather in large colonies to mate and raise their chicks.

Emperors don't make nests. The mother lays the egg on her feet. It's a big egg. It weighs about a pound. Carefully she passes it to the father. Then she heads back to the sea for food.

With winter approaching, even more ice forms over the ocean. This makes it a longer walk back to the

An emperor penguin glides over the snow, "tobogganing" to its destination.

A group of emperor penguins huddle together for warmth in frigid Antarctica.

The "baby-sitter" of this crèche of emperor penguins stands guard over the young penguins while their parents travel to the sea for food.

water, sometimes 50 miles (80 kilometers). She may not walk the whole way. Penguins have another way to travel. They get down on their bellies and "toboggan" over the ice, pushing themselves with their flippers.

Meanwhile, the father penguin incubates the egg. He holds it on his feet, and keeps it warm under a special flap of feathery skin called a brood patch. Every so often he turns the egg around so that all parts of it get the warmth from his body. This helps the egg to develop properly.

By now it's the coldest time of year, in the coldest place on Earth. There are winds of 100 miles (161 kilometers) an hour. The temperature can drop to minus 76°F (–60°C). It is dark twenty-four hours a day. The father penguins huddle together on the ice and share their body heat. They shuffle around—each with an egg on his feet—shifting positions so that no one has to stand at the cold outer edge of the group for too long.

Two months go by before the mothers return. They have spent much of that time traveling back and forth over the ice. Now it's the father's turn to go to the sea. He passes the egg back to its mother.

The egg hatches, and the new chick sits on its mother's feet. It sticks its beak into her mouth, and she feeds it regurgitated food she has carried back in her stomach. The chick stays cozy and warm under its mother's flap of belly skin. Even if the egg hatches a few days *before* the food-filled mother returns, the father penguin manages to bring up a bit of food for the chick from his almost-starved body. Remember, by now he hasn't eaten for three or four months. He has been living off his body fat, and has lost about half his weight.

After a while, the chick joins a crèche. Now both parents can go for food at the same time. This is important, because as the chick gets bigger, it needs more and more

> ## How to identify an emperor penguin
>
> (*Aptenodytes forsteri*):
>
> Long, black down-curved beak, black feet, black head. Has more feathers and longer feathers than any other penguin. Even its beak has feathers.
>
> Height: 35 inches
> (89 centimeters)
>
> Weight: up to 90 pounds
> (41 kilograms)

food. The penguins travel back and forth over the ice. If you were there, you would see two processions—one heading toward the water, one coming back with food.

It takes four or five months before the emperor chicks shed their fluffy down and are equipped with waterproof feathers. It's a shorter walk to the sea now. Winter is ending. It's getting warmer, and much of the sea ice has melted. The older penguins stay back on the ice for about a month while they molt—another long time when they must go without food.

When summer comes, the entire group goes into the sea—where they swim, dive, eat their fill, and fatten up—till autumn. Then, once again the emperor penguins make their way back to their breeding ground on the sea ice. And the whole cycle begins again, as it has for millions of years.

Emperor penguins, along with king penguins, are in the genus GIANT PENGUINS.

Some chinstraps and gentoos also nest on the Antarctic Peninsula, which juts up toward the north and is not as cold as the rest of the continent.

Why do the Antarctic penguins keep going back to such a harsh and uninviting part of the world?

The answer lies in the past.

Antarctica was not always covered with ice and snow. Millions of years ago it was a warmer place, covered with forests of giant ferns. Dinosaurs and other prehistoric creatures lived there 150 million years ago. We know this because fossils of the dinosaurs hypsilophodon and ankylosaur have been found there—as well as fossils of an even earlier reptile called Lystrosaurus, which once roamed in great herds over the area that is now Antarctica.

Back then, Antarctica was not a separate continent. It was part of a supercontinent we call Gondwanaland, made up of areas that are now Africa, India, South America, Australia, and Antarctica. About 160 million years ago, the supercontinent began to split up. Parts of it "drifted," over millions of years, to their present locations. This process, called "continental drift," continues today.

Penguins have existed for at least 50 million years. Prehistoric penguins were similar to the penguins of today, except that some were super-sized: 5 to 6 feet (1.5 to 2 meters) tall, weighing about 250 pounds (113 kilograms). We can tell from the fossils that, even then, penguins didn't fly. They had flippers. And their bones were solid and heavy—suitable for swimming and diving, but not for flying.

Prehistoric **PENGUINS**

Scientists tell us that penguins are descended from earlier birds that *did* fly. But by 50 million years ago, they had already become adapted to life in the sea, and had evolved to their present form.

When penguins first started nesting in Antarctica, the climate was probably like New Zealand's today. As it got colder, the penguins—already equipped with their layers of fat and warm feathers—were able to adapt even further and survive in the new conditions. The feathers of Antarctic penguins are longer, warmer, and more closely packed than feathers of other penguins. (Up to 300 feathers per square inch.) They also have super-thick layers of fat under their skin.

There are some advantages to Antarctica. The surrounding sea is rich with food—fish, squid, and masses of pink, shrimplike krill. Also, there are no land predators.

When early explorers from Europe saw penguins for the first time, they were puzzled. What *were* these things? Fish with feathers? Furry sea creatures?

Whatever they were, the seamen were happy to find them, for a very practical reason. After their long sea voyage, supplies were low. The crew was often in desperate need of food. Penguins were easy to kill. The meat was salted and could be preserved for months. Penguin eggs were also gathered.

In 1594, Sir Richard Hawkins wrote:

The flesh of these Pengwins is much of the savour of a certain Fowle . . . which we call Puffins . . . . They are very fat . . . they are reasonable meate rosted, baked or sodden; but best rosted . . . . We salted some dozen or sixteene Hogsheads [big barrels] *which served us . . . insteed of . . . Beefe.*

Some of the explorers and traders viewed the penguins as more than just a handy, fast-food supply. They became fascinated by the birds themselves. Their descriptions tell us that they were good nature-watchers.

In 1620, Admiral Beauleau noted:

. . . The Pinguins are Fowls without Wings, which have two Fins, and two broad Paws, upon which they walk upright, and with which they dig the Ground to make their Nests . . . . In the morning they repair to the Sea, where they swim and feed upon Fish, and at night return to their Nests . . . . for my part, I take them to be feather'd Fish.

PENGUINS
and People

The traders soon thought of more reasons to go after the easy-to-kill birds. Their colorful plumes could be used to decorate hats, their feathers to stuff mattresses, and their skins to make slippers and purses. Egg-gathering also became a big industry. In one year 300,000 eggs were taken from Dassan Island, off the coast of Africa.

Then, it was discovered that penguin fat was a good source of oil. Penguin-oil factories were built on South Georgia Island, Macquarie Island, and other nesting areas. Millions of penguins were thrown into huge vats and boiled down for oil. In 1867, one company alone boiled down about 400,000 king penguins to get 50,000 gallons of oil.

If this had continued, there probably would now be no penguins in the world. Luckily, oil wells became a better source of oil than penguins. Also, as people began to learn more about the cruelty involved in the penguin-oil business, they objected to it. In the 1980s, when a company wanted permission to kill penguins at Punta Tombo for oil, food, and leather, people in Argentina protested. As a result, a law was passed forbidding the killing of penguins in Argentina. All penguin species, worldwide, are now protected. Does this mean that penguins are safe from harm?

Some penguin species are thriving. There are more than 15 million chinstraps, more than 25 million macaronis, about 4 million rockhoppers, and 2 million king penguins. But some other species—Humboldts, Galápagos, and yellow-eyed penguins—are in real danger of becoming extinct.

Penguins have always faced natural threats, such as predators, disease, floods, and scarcity of food. When these things occur, many penguins die. But the setback is temporary, and after a while their numbers increase once again.

What is most threatening to penguins today are human activities. And these do not come and go in cycles. They are ongoing. And so the penguins have no time to recoup their losses, as they do from natural threats.

What are some of the indirect ways in which humans harm penguins? Oil pollution is one. A penguin with feathers gummed together by oil can't survive. The penguins that suffer most from this are African black-footed penguins. The waters they swim in are on a route taken by oil supertankers. There are accidental spills. Oil is often deliberately flushed from tankers. One spill killed thousands of black-footed penguins.

Loss of habitat is another threat. This problem has almost wiped out the yellow-eyed penguins. New Zealand rain forests, where these penguins once nested, have been cut down for lumber and for farms and pas-

The PENGUINS' FUTURE

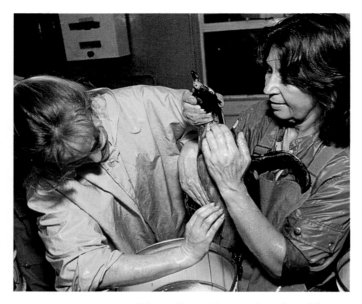

Near Cape Town, South Africa, a black-footed penguin is cleaned up after its rescue from an oil slick.

tures. The number of yellow-eyed penguins is now very low. If a large protected habitat is not set aside for them, they will soon be extinct—gone from the earth forever.

Many penguins drown when they get tangled up in large driftnets used for fishing. There are groups in Australia working to stop the use of driftnets. Overfishing—catching too many fish, too fast—also means the loss of the penguins' food supply.

When we take steps to protect penguins and other wildlife, it does not mean we are taking benefits away from people. Very often, the opposite is true. Usually, what helps wildlife helps human life as well.

Penguins have been on Earth for millions of years. Let's hope that they can continue to survive in all of their varieties, in all of their habitats. It's up to us. More and more people see that we have a lot to gain in sharing the Earth with the many interesting forms of life that are different from ourselves—including those peppy, scrappy, most unusual birds, the penguins.

FOR *Further* **READING**

Berger, Melvin. *Oil Spill!* New York: HarperCollins, 1994.

Davis, Lloyd S. *Penguin: A Season in the Life of the Adélie Penguin.* San Diego: Harcourt, Brace, 1994.

McMillan, Bruce. *Penguins at Home: Gentoos of Antarctica.* Boston: Houghton Mifflin, 1993.

McMillan, Bruce. *Summer Ice: Antarctic Life.* San Diego: Houghton Mifflin, 1995.

Myers, Christopher A., and Myers, Lynne Born. *Galápagos: Islands of Change.* New York: Hyperion, 1995.

Patent, Dorothy Hinshaw. *Looking at Penguins.* New York: Holiday House, 1993.

Poncet, Sally. *South Georgia.* New York: Simon and Schuster, 1995.

Sømme, Lauritz, and Kalas, Sybille. *The Penguin Family Book.* New York: North-South Books, 1995.

Wexo, John Bonnet. *Penguins.* Mankato, MN: Creative Education, 1989.

Index